# Sitting Meditation in Won Buddhism

# Sitting Meditation in Won Buddhism
Digging to the Roots

## Serge V. Yarovoi

Balboa Press
A Division of Hay House,
1663 Liberty Drive,
Bloomington, IN 47403,
www.balboapress.com
1-(877) 407-4847

Copyright © 2012 Serge V. Yarovoi

All rights reserved. No part of this book may be used or reproduced by any means, graphic, electronic, or mechanical, including photocopying, recording, taping or by any information storage retrieval system without the written permission of the publisher except in the case of brief quotations embodied in critical articles and reviews.

ISBN: 978-1-4525-5635-2 (sc)
ISBN: 978-1-4525-5634-5 (e)

Library of Congress Control Number: 2012914044

Balboa Press books may be ordered through booksellers or by contacting:

Balboa Press
A Division of Hay House
1663 Liberty Drive
Bloomington, IN 47403
www.balboapress.com
1-(877) 407-4847

Grateful acknowledgment is made to reprint the following:

From *The Foundations of Chinese Medicine. A Comprehensive Text for Acupuncturists and Herbalists* by G. Maciocia published by Elsevier, 2005. All rights reserved. Reprinted with permission of publisher.

From *Hara: The Vital Center of Man* by Karlfried Graf Dürckheim published by Inner Traditions, a division of Inner Traditions International, 2004. All rights reserved. http://www.Innertraditions.com Reprinted with permission of publisher.

From *Taoist Meditation*, translated by Thomas Cleary, ©2000 by Thomas Cleary. Reprinted by arrangement with Shambhala Publications Inc., Boston, MA. www.shambhala.com.

From *The Scriptures of Won-Buddhism: A Translation of the Wonbulgyo kyojon with Introduction* by Bongkil Chung, published by A Kuroda Institute Book, Honolulu, Hawaii: University of Hawaii Press, 2003. All rights reserved. Reprinted with permission of publisher.

From 원불교 출판사, 전북 익산시 신용동 344-2 원불교 중앙총부, 2006 지은이: 이광정. *[Commentary on the Method of Sitting Meditation in Chungjeon, 3rd edition, by Ven. Chwasan.]* Published by Won Kwang Publishing Co., 2006. All rights reserved. Reprinted with permission of publisher.

Because of the dynamic nature of the Internet, any web addresses or links contained in this book may have changed since publication and may no longer be valid. The views expressed in this work are solely those of the author and do not necessarily reflect the views of the publisher, and the publisher hereby disclaims any responsibility for them.

The author of this book does not dispense medical advice or prescribe the use of any technique as a form of treatment for physical, emotional, or medical problems without the advice of a physician, either directly or indirectly. The intent of the author is only to offer information of a general nature to help you in your quest for emotional and spiritual wellbeing. In the event you use any of the information in this book for yourself, which is your constitutional right, the author and the publisher assume no responsibility for your actions.

Any people depicted in stock imagery provided by Thinkstock are models, and such images are being used for illustrative purposes only.
Certain stock imagery © Thinkstock.

Printed in the United States of America

Balboa Press rev. date: 8/9/2012

*To my mother and my family, the advanced human beings who have taught me a lot and who make my life complete.*

*You, indeed, are the master of yourself.*
*You, indeed, are your own refuge.*

The Dhammapada, Ch. 25, 'The Practitioner'

# Contents

Preface ..................................................................... *viii*
Acknowledgments................................................... *ix*
Introduction............................................................. 1
Chapter 1. The Instructions for Meditation in Won Buddhism... 3
Chapter 2. The Founding of Won Buddhism and its Historical
 Backgrounds................................................. 5
Chapter 3. The Need for Resting in the Elixir Field................ 12
Chapter 4. The Method of Sitting in Meditation.................. 15
Chapter 5. The Benefits of Meditation: Won Buddhism Instructions
 and Contemporary Studies on Meditation................. 33
Afterword................................................................ 37
Notes..................................................................... 38
Bibliography........................................................... 39
Index..................................................................... 42
About the Author.................................................... 48

# PREFACE

This research was originally undertaken out of the author's curiosity and sincere interest in the forms, methods, and historical sources of sitting meditation practices as they are currently practiced in Korean Won Buddhism. The seeming simplicity of the meditation techniques used in Won Buddhism should not be misunderstood as artificial efforts to simplify more elaborate practices; rather, they are the result of thorough selection of the methods historically proven to be the most effective for generations of practitioners.

This research was used by the author as a Master's degree thesis in the Applied Meditation Program at the Won Institute of Graduate Studies in Glenside, PA.

Among the plethora of ancient and modern texts devoted to the subject of meditation, the author focused mainly on texts for which an English translation was available. This makes sources referenced in this book accessible to Western readers, most of whom do not have knowledge of Eastern languages.

Certainly, the bibliography in this book is far from covering the subject and is by no means exhaustive. It is merely the author's invitation for interested readers to undertake their own adventure – to travel back into the literary past and discover for themselves the wisdom of the great masters of the Eastern contemplative traditions.

# ACKNOWLEDGEMENTS

Over the years of my meditation practice and studies, I have received invaluable support, inspiration, and encouragement from many people who play an important role in my life and who shared with me their wisdom, sincerity, and knowledge.

My deep appreciation goes to the people who played a critical role in my spiritual development and personal growth – some of them as teachers, others as my family members, close friends, or fellow students in the Applied Meditation Studies program, and some of them in several of these roles. Without them, my meditation studies, including this book, would not be possible.

My special thanks are due to all (in alphabetical order) whose direct or indirect contributions to this book were absolutely essential:

Armstrong, Guy
Cines, Douglas B.
Craven, Carole
Dallery, Carlton
Goldstein, Joseph
Ha, Chung Nam
Hwang, Sangwon
Insight Meditation Society, Barr, MA
Kim, Bokin
Koh, Yoon Suk
Logvinenko, Evgeny
My Family
Rocco, Gabriel
Rosen, Helen J.
Sa, Youngin
Salzberg, Sharon
Song, Seung Hyeun
Wallis, Glenn
Won Buddhism Temple Sangha in Glenside, PA
Won Institute of Graduate Studies, Glenside, PA
Yoo, Moojin

I would like to express my thanks to all of them for their suggestions, advice, discussions, and disagreements when such were necessary. It is from disagreements that I have learned the most.

x

# INTRODUCTION

The practitioners of any meditation system, including those of Buddhist meditation, have a variety of contemplative practices to choose from. At first glance, it may appear that some of those practices are mutually exclusive: Some are simple while others are elaborate; some require active involvement of all the senses while others just teach us to "shut off" any kind of conventional perceptions; and some are easy to practice for a vast majority of people while others may require an experienced teacher and a lifelong dedication to master.

From those unlimited techniques and methods, informed and thoughtful practitioners can find their own approaches depending on their level of understanding and eagerness, personal inclinations and preferences, and lifestyle and life goals.

For the inquisitive mind, the readings on and comparative analysis of the various meditation techniques and approaches could be not less breathtaking than the reading of a detective novel. Digging to the roots of meditation practice may reveal to readers the heroes and villains of the story, the colorful decorations surrounding the characters on the stage, and the hidden mechanisms working silently behind the scene. Readers may experience some of those "aha!" moments when they find, often in unexpected places, the fingerprints of the subject under investigation, sometimes worn off and mutilated by time past but still quite recognizable under the microscope of the investigator's curiosity.

After being introduced to the Won Buddhism version of sitting meditation, the author was intrigued by the abundance of apparently non-Buddhist inclusions into the instructions for meditation in the Scriptures of Won Buddhism. This book came to life as a result of the author's attempts to investigate the sources and origins of such inclusions.

As in a variety of other oriental traditions of meditation practice, the fundamental aim of sitting meditation in Won Buddhism is to nurture and develop the basic spirit of human beings.

Sitting Won Buddhism meditation is typically practiced in tranquility, for it is important for one's mind to not be aroused by daily activities. Notably, however, the practice of calm sitting meditation in Won Buddhism must be necessarily balanced and done hand in hand with the practice called "timeless Zen," which consists of constant mindfulness throughout the day. This book, however, will concentrate only on the sitting meditation aspect of Won Buddhist teachings.

Before anything else, it should be noted that the followers of Won Buddhism teachings are to achieve this goal by mastering the skill of concentrating their energy at the *Tanjon* or *Danjeon* (Dan Tian, Tantien, or Dandien in Chinese; Chung, 2003, p. 145). The Tanjon technique that is accepted in Won Buddhism is *not* a commonly accepted meditation technique in the Buddhist tradition.

The Scriptures of Won Buddhism contain explicit instructions for sitting meditation in "Chapter Four: Sitting in Meditation" under "Part Three: Practice" of *The Canon* (Chung, 2003, p. 145). The instructions are straightforward to follow yet thorough and carefully detailed. They explain the purport, the method, and the merits of meditation and the necessity of concentrating at the "elixir field," Tanjon. Because the methods for practicing meditation stipulated by the instructions are simultaneously simple and sufficient, we were intrigued to trace their meaning, their history, and at least some of their sources. Why did Sot'aesan (1891–1943, born Pak Chung-Bin), the founder of Won Buddhism, give preference to these easy and clear methods over the myriad other approaches to meditation? To what other methods and techniques are Sot'aesan's guidelines related? How did Sot'aesan's life, environment, and historical context influence his choice of meditation practice?

We will show here how, through deep theoretical and experiential studies, through a selection of multiple Buddhist and non-Buddhist sources, and through a robust approach to meditation practice, informed by the knowledge of the lay majority's needs as well as a clear understanding of the advantages and restrictions of each separate practice, Sot'aesan completed the monumental task of creating the instructions for meditation in Won Buddhism.

Understanding the scope of the task, the author does not even hope to paint the complete and fully detailed picture and asks that his work be considered simply as his rather modest attempt to approach the subject. He would be grateful to his readers for any additions, suggestions, or critiques sent to **wontechnique@gmail.com**

Before anything else, we should turn to the history of Won Buddhism, as well as to Sot'aesan's personal history, to determine the answer to—or at least take a step toward answering—some of the questions above. We assume that the best way to understand Sot'aesan's choice of meditation practice is to analyze both the historical context of his work and the explanations given in the Scriptures of Won Buddhism itself.

# Chapter 1
# The Instructions for Meditation in Won Buddhism

There are several translations of the Scriptures of Won Buddhism into English. Unless stated otherwise, we will use *The Scriptures of Won Buddhism: A Translation of the Wonbulgyo Kyojon with Introduction* by Bongkil Chung (2003) for all discussions. In this translation, we find the following instructions for meditation:

**Part Three: Practice**
*Chapter Four: Sitting in Meditation*

*I. The Purport*
*Sitting in meditation is a practice the purpose of which is to calm delusive thoughts and allow the true nature of one's mind to manifest. It is also a practice to make the fiery energy descend and the watery energy ascend in one's body. As delusive thoughts calm down, the watery energy will ascend in the body; as the watery energy ascends, delusive thoughts calm down. Consequently, one's mental and physical functioning will be consistent, and one will feel both the spirit and the vital force refreshed.*

*If, however, delusive thoughts persist in one's mind, the fiery energy will constantly ascend, burning up the watery energy in the body and covering up the light of the spirit. The human body functions like a steam engine; not even a finger can be moved without the dual force of fire and water. Since the six sense organs are all controlled by the brain and hence the fiery energy of the whole body is contracted there when one uses the six roots to see, hear, or think, the watery energy of the whole body is dried and burned there as the oil in the lamp is burned when it is lit. One's face flushes and one's mouth dries out if one racks one's brain, looks minutely at a thing, or talks loudly; this is the phenomenon of the ascending fiery energy. One should use one's six sense organs with frugality even for rightful things; why should one let useless delusive thoughts burn the flame of the brain day and night? Thus, sitting in meditation is a practice to remove all delusive thoughts, to let the original nature of True Thusness[1] manifest, to have all the fiery energy descend, and to let the clear and pure watery energy ascend.*

## II. The Method

*The method of sitting in meditation is very simple and easy; anyone can practice it.*

1. Sit on a mat comfortably; hold your head and back straight in an upright, seated posture.[2]

2. Loosen the tension of the body and gather it at the elixir field (tanjon); be aware only of the physical energy concentrated at the elixir field with no thought dwelling anywhere. If your mind is unguarded, the energy loses concentration. If that happens, do not forget to check the concentration of energy.

3. Keep your breathing uniform, inhaling a little longer and stronger than exhaling.

4. To keep the demon of drowsiness away, keep your eyes open; however, you may try with your eyes closed if you feel refreshed as long as there is no danger of drowsiness.

5. Keep your mouth always closed. If the ascent of the watery energy and the descent of the fiery energy go well as the practice matures, clear and smooth saliva will flow from the salivary gland, which you may gather in the mouth and swallow once in a while.

6. Let your spirit be wakeful in calmness and calm in wakefulness; if you become drowsy, collect your mind to freshen the spirit; if your mind turns to delusive thoughts, replace them with right thought; then stay in the realm of the True Thusness of your original nature.

7. The beginner at sitting in meditation sometimes suffers from pain in the legs and the invasion of delusive thoughts. If your legs ache, you may change their positions, one upon the other. If delusive thoughts invade your mind, recognize them only as delusive thoughts; then they will disappear of themselves. Do not be vexed with or discouraged by them.

8. If you sit in meditation for the first time, your face and body may feel itchy occasionally as if ants were crawling over them. Be sure not to touch or scratch. This is the symptom of the blood passing through the blood vessels.

9. While sitting in meditation, do not search for any extraordinary pivotal point or any miraculous traces; should you notice such phenomena, recognize them as wicked and pass over them as nothing worthy of attention.

If you practice sitting in meditation for a long time as described above, you will eventually forget the distinction between subject and object, time and place, remaining in the realm of the True Thusness of your original nature and rejoicing in unparalleled spiritual bliss.

# CHAPTER 2
# THE FOUNDING OF WON BUDDHISM AND ITS HISTORICAL BACKGROUNDS

Now that we are already familiar with the instructions for meditation as it exists in Won Buddhism, we wish to discuss the historical context in which Sot'aesan, the founder of Won Buddhism, created the foundation of a reformed Buddhist movement in Korea. Before we read too far into the instructions above, we should clearly see the "basement" on which the movement was built.

Robert Buswell, Jr., a distinguished professor of Korean and Chinese Buddhist studies and the director of the Center for Buddhist Studies at the University of California, Los Angeles (UCLA), informs us thus (p.157):

> *Among the most prominent of [reform movements in Korea] was Won Buddhism, founded in 1916 by Sot'aesan (1891-1943), which combined Buddhist teaching with a disparate variety of elements drawn from Confucianism, Taoism, Tonghak³, and even Christianity.*

In 1916, Sot'aesan originated a reformed Buddhist movement (Park, 2003, pp. 169–194). The movement was later named Won Buddhism (*Wonbulgyo* in Korean) by his successor, Song Kyu (1900–1962), who is better known as the Second Head Dharma Master Chongsan.

The notion that Sot'aesan, who gave his preference to the Buddha Dharma and believed that the Buddha's wisdom and power are unlimited, made reforming Buddhism in Korea a lifetime goal may initially seem strange. It is to be remarked, however, that according to the opinion generally accepted in Won Buddhism, Sot'aesan attained great enlightenment entirely through his own efforts and without the guidance of any teacher in his search for truth. Only subsequently did he begin to see himself as a Buddhist, regard the Buddha as his original teacher, and merge the Buddha's teachings with his own ideas. In other words, it was not until after his enlightenment that he incorporated, used, and made reference to the traditional Buddhist teachings, ideas, and concepts such as sitting meditation without *koan* versus *koan*-observing meditation. It is not surprising, then, that the Buddhist teachings reformed by Sot'aesan have many original, distinctive aspects while retaining the essence of traditional Buddhism.

After his reading of the Diamond Sūtra soon after his enlightenment, Sot'aesan saw a very natural relationship between the traditional Buddhist teachings and his own religious approach, which was based on his unique experience of coming to enlightenment. Holding the teachings of the Buddha Śākyamuni to be the most profound and, hence, superior to all other doctrines, Sot'aesan deemed the Buddha Śākyamuni to be the "sage of all sages" and lauded his teachings. To Sot'aesan, nothing could rival the immensity and the profoundness of the Buddha. Recognizing the Buddhist principles as the cornerstone of his own teachings was therefore quite natural for him. His confidence that Buddhism would be the most practiced religion in the world likewise shows his fondness for Buddhism.

All in all, it can be said that Sot'aesan had given the Buddha's teachings a central role in his own religious system (Scripture of Sot'aesan, *Taejonggyong 1.2*, in Chung, 2003, p. 167). At the same time, however, Sot'aesan was a reformer. He envisioned that the Buddha Dharma of the future would differ from that of the past (Scripture of Sot'aesan, *Taejonggyong 1.15*, in Chung, 2003, pp. 172–173), a concept that attracted those looking for change to his novel doctrine.

Simultaneously with all his reverence for Buddhism and the Buddhist teachings, Sot'aesan considered Buddhism in Korea to be an imported religion having a distinctly non-Korean intellectual heritage. Between 1919 and 1924, he advanced his opinions about reforming Korean Buddhism in conversations with Korean monks. When his ideas received rather little response, he decided to take on the task of overhauling Korean Buddhism from outside of the traditional Korean monastic system.

Sot'aesan's reformation began in 1924 with the formation of the Research Society of the Buddha Dharma (*Pulbop yon'guhoe* in Korean), a religious organization that became a new religious movement. In 1947, the movement was renamed Won Buddhism.

Sot'aesan made the Buddhist teachings more fitting and helpful for the times. He emphasized all throughout that Buddhism should be practiced by majority of the people, whether they be clergy or laypeople, a course of action that showed his veneration for the Buddha Dharma. According to Sot'aesan, Buddhism just needed to be updated because the overall archaic, imported monastic system, together with a number of old doctrines, produced problems in modern-day Korean society. He was quite clear that the chief principles of traditional Buddhism would still be preserved; his religious modernization would be no more or less than a contemporary strain of Buddhism.

The concept of skillful means (*upaya* in Sanskrit) was the general idea underlying Sot'aesan's reformation of the monastic system and the Buddhist practice in Korea. He believed Buddhist systems and the Buddha's teachings to be the skillful-means that had to be correctly applied to present-day Korean society. Throughout all his plans to reform Buddhism, Sot'aesan always preserved the idea of updating some Buddhist doctrines and the entire monastic system without deviating from the core principles of Buddhism.

The most important intent of Sot'aesan's reformation of Buddhism, according to Sot'aesan himself, was to spread Buddhist thought from the monasteries in the mountains to the general public to enable Buddhism to be fully practiced and applied in present-day nonreligious society. Since the main barrier to achieving this goal was the difficulty laypeople faced in understanding the presentation of Buddhist concepts, Sot'aesan made having Buddhism accessible a definite priority.

Originated in India circa the sixth century BCE, Buddhism was introduced to Korea through China near the end of the fourth century CE. Despite the length of time that had passed since then, Sot'aesan held that Buddhism in Korea remained a borrowed, foreign religion. More than fifteen hundred years had somehow not been enough to integrate Buddhism seamlessly into the Korean culture. For instance, if the Korean general populace attempted to read the Buddhist scriptures, they would come across many unfamiliar terms of Indian and Chinese origins that were not understandable to common Koreans. Whether one was learned or ignorant, intelligent or dim-witted, it was difficult for him or her who was outside the monastic system to grasp the Buddha's teachings. Because of this situation, Sot'aesan thought that any existing variety of Buddhism—whether traditional Korean Buddhism, Chinese Buddhism, or Indian Buddhism—would not and could not be influential in society. He saw this situation as needing correction.

As a first measure, Sot'aesan suggested the somewhat arduous work of producing introductory books and references on Buddhism (Sotaesan, 1997, p. 296) in the Korean language.

Sot'aesan himself provided guidelines for the selection of Korean Buddhist literature for further use. He also emphasized the importance of realizing these works in a simple, straightforward style using Korean expressions and names to make the teachings of the Buddha more accessible.

The goal was always one and the same: to bring the teachings of the Buddha into a context where they could be understood by the common Korean populace. Sot'aesan's planned creation of introductory literature would be one of the many steps taken to fulfill that goal (Sot'aesan, 1997, p. 296).

Unsurprisingly enough, most of Sot'aesan's own writings were also published in Korean and employed but a small number of Chinese idiomatic expressions.

It is necessary to comprehend that during the Choson dynasty (1392–1910), there formed two schools of Korean Buddhism: the Doctrinal School, also known as the Orthodox School, and the Meditation-Only School. The former grouped around Buddhist scholarship, and a fair number of highly eminent monks expanded it quite quickly. The main streams of Buddhist scholastic thought were imported to Korea from China during the period of the Three Kingdoms, in 372 CE. The Doctrinal School had a great variety of branches, or subschools, the Buddhist commentaries and scriptures of many of which were introduced to the courts of Koguryŏ (traditionally dated 37 BCE–668 CE) and Paekche (traditionally dated 18 BCE–660 CE), two of the three great kingdoms.

The subschools differed in opinions as far as which Buddhist scriptures they considered the most essential. For instance, the school of the Three Treatises is grouped around the following three treatises: the *Mādhyamika Śāstra (Treatise of Treatises)* of Nāgārjuna (ca. 150–250 CE), the *Dvadasanikāya Śāstra (Twelve Gates Treatise)* of Nāgārjuna also, and the *Śata Śāstra (One Hundred Verses Treatise)* of Āryadeva (third century CE). The T'en-tai school that was founded during the Suei dynasty (589–618), on the other hand, chose the Lotus Sūtra as the most important scripture; the Huayan (Hua-yen) school (ca. 600–700 CE) opted for the *Avataṃsaka Sūtra (Mahāvaipulya Buddhāvataṃsaka Sūtra, Flower Garland Sūtra)*.

Sot'aesan thought that to fully comprehend the Buddha's power and wisdom, the teachings of the different Doctrinal schools and the Meditation-Only School had to be combined. Talking about Sot'aesan, we can repeat what Robert E. Buswell, Jr., said (1986, p. 200) about another great Korean charismatic reformer of Buddhism, Chinul (1158–1210):

> [He] *was able to see the value and utility in each of the two major aspects of Buddhist spiritual endeavor - doctrinal study and meditation practice – and to develop an approach to religious cultivation that drew upon both.*

To Sot'aesan, each school represented but a fragment of the Buddha's teachings, and in meditation practice, even if some schools taught multiple methods, these schools had a tendency to restrict the subjects taught to lay devotees to one or two of the following:

1) Scripture study
2) Sitting meditation aided by *hwadu*
3) Intoning the name of a Buddha, or other incantation
4) Buddhist offering

Like his great predecessor Chinul, Sot'aesan believed that the only way to realize the depth and the full meaning of the Buddha's teachings was to combine all of the above practices. He argued for the necessity of each practice (Sot'aesan, 1997, pp. 298–299).

Sot'aesan held that when people learned only some of these methods, they tended to argue and disagree with others. He thought of aiding people in understanding the whole immensity of Buddhism by merging the separate schools into one cohesive practice. To this end, he adopted the three major attributes of the Buddhist practice: wisdom, meditation, and morality.

In Buddhism, the three practices are known as Threefold Training. Sot'aesan adopted and reformulated the Threefold Training of Buddhism to become the Gate of Practice, or Discipline, in Won Buddhism. However, his system also expands upon the Threefold Training and gives specific guidelines for practicing each of the three practices: meditation, wisdom, and morality. Sot'aesan's version of the Threefold Training consists of Cultivation of Spirituality, Contemplation into Facts and Principles, and Choosing Mindful Actions.

Sot'aesan did not believe that there is one exclusive way to carry out these practices; his attitude toward meditation was quite pragmatic. He held that all these divergent practices could function together and be adapted to the different needs and capacities of practitioners according to their levels of spiritual development.

During the Tang dynasty, two mainstream schools still in existence today were originated in China as the Cáodòng (Ts'ao-tung) and Línji (Lin-chi) schools (Japanese Sōtō and Rinzai, respectively). According to them, meditation practice is done either through just wholehearted sitting, the Sōtō school's method, or through practicing koans (*kungan* in Ch'an), the Rinzai school's primary method.

Sot'aesan admitted the validity of the Rinzai approach to meditation (Scripture of Sot'aesan, *Taejonggyong 1.19*, in Chung, 2003, p. 177): "*The purpose of sitting in kanhwa meditation is to help one become enlightened to the profound truth, which is difficult to teach by scriptures or verbal explanations.*"

However, Sot'aesan felt that the Sōtō approach is more appropriate for the great majority of lay practitioners, who are simply not interested in enlightenment or *koan* practice. In his view, meditation time and *koan* studies should be separated (Scripture of Sot'aesan, *Taejonggyong 3.14*, in Chung, 2003, p. 202):

> *The Master said to an assembly at a Zen Monastery, "In recent years, proponents of various sects of Zen Buddhism argue with each other on the correctness of each method. In this order I have adopted the method of concentration at the elixir field so that one should exclusively practice mental concentration for spiritual cultivation while practicing the seated meditation; and the exercise with hwadu should be done only once in a while at a proper time. The reason is that the awakening does not occur only at the end of a long mental wrestling with uidu in a depressed frame of mind; the power of uidu exercise in a clear spirit at the right moment is superior."*

After examining all the scriptures of the Doctrinal schools and all the *kongans* of the Zen school, Sot'aesan chose the most important of them as the practices that could be used to achieve the Power of Inquiry into Facts and Principles (wisdom, *prajñā* in Sanskrit). Once again showing his commitment to simplifying Buddhism for the benefit of the masses, he filtered out complex scriptures and *kongans* during this process. Wisdom was therefore to be reached by following the most basic precepts of the Buddha Dharma. The Cultivation of Spirituality could be helped along by practices such as intoning the name of a Buddha or speaking other incantations while sitting in meditation. The precepts, the practice of the Way of the Fourfold Beneficence, and the knowledge of the principle of karmic retribution would allow one to achieve Mindful Choice in Action.

Sot'aesan believed that these Three Great Practices should be learned hand in hand by all devotees. The practices of Inquiry, Cultivation, and Mindful Choice would enable each devotee's acquisition of, respectively, the Buddha's Power of Inquiry (*prajñā* in Sanskrit), which consists of the ability to see principles and truths without obstruction; Power of Meditation (*samādhi* in Sanskrit), which keeps one from becoming attached to the things of this world; and Power of Mindful Choice (*śīla* in Sanskrit), which permits one to differentiate right from wrong and execute the right action (Sot'aesan, 1997, p. 299).

Establishing his organization in reaction to the monk-centric systems and doctrines of the Buddhist *Saṃgha*, Sot'aesan was eager to teach his disciples as intensively as possible regardless of what their gender or social status might be. During the period when his religious reformation was just budding, he trained his disciples at night and worked with them during the day. He held his first intensive training in meditation, which lasted a month, at Mandok Mountain in Chinan, North Cholla Province, in May 1924. Both his male and female disciples as well as their children completed this intensive meditation program. In March 1925, a year later, he gave the name Fixed-Term and Daily Training to this training program, all of whose attendees would receive highly intensive training during its entire duration.

Disciples trained themselves as instructed by the Six Articles to Heed in Daily Applications and the Six Articles to Heed While Attending the Temple throughout the Daily Training (Chung, 2003, pp. 141–142).

It is well-known that Sot'aesan's selection of useful methods and techniques was not restricted solely to Buddhist sources. In his search for the truth, he studied not only the Eastern sources, like Taoist, Confucian, and *Ch'ondogyo*[4] scriptures and commentaries but also sources as distant as the Christian Old and New Testaments (Scripture of Sot'aesan, *Taejonggyong*, in Chung, 2003, p. 167). In fact, his scriptures, in their structure and text organization, resemble the Christian New Testament more than they resemble the traditional Buddhist documents. Everything potentially useful and important was thoroughly studied by Sot'aesan, analyzed and selected, and then meticulously organized into a clear, easy-to-follow system. Meditation is one of the most fundamental concepts in this reformed Buddhist system.

Although Sot'aesan did not necessarily reject all aspects of shamanism or Taoism (as discussed below), he desired to avoid having himself or his followers misclassified as shamanic because he thought it important to avoid any misunderstanding regarding the nature of his reforms. Introducing ancient pre-Buddhist practices in his teachings, he wished it to be understood that his religious activities have the goal of teaching and practicing the Buddha Dharma.

After introducing this historical background, it is time to turn to the methods of meditation selected, among others, by the Founding Head Dharma Master of Won Buddhism, Sot'aesan.

# CHAPTER 3
# THE NEED FOR RESTING IN THE ELIXIR FIELD

As we already pointed out, the Tanjon technique in Won Buddhism is a distinctive and not commonly accepted meditation technique in Buddhist tradition. Some masters, however, even recommend considering it as the center of the universe while meditating—that is how powerful it is.

One should be reminded that the Tanjon is not a fixed anatomical location in the body but rather the center of gravity and the location from where a person's vital energy is distributed throughout the organism.

To Westerners, the Tanjon is better known in its Japanese term, *hara*, meaning "belly." However, as will be discussed later, the word *hara* is used in Japanese not only in the narrow meaning usually meant by Western people but also in a more important, much wider, and more philosophical existential context. The words *fukubu, o-naka* (the honored middle), *and kikai* are also used to mean "belly" in Japanese; the last term plays a certain part in connection with Tanden, the Japanese pronunciation for Tanjon, which refers to the body's center of gravity. This same location is also referred to as the "elixir field" in ancient Chinese Taoist sources as well as, subsequently, in the Scriptures of Won Buddhism. As in Taoism, in Won Buddhism, the Tanjon is described as a spot located in the lower abdomen, approximately two and a half inches below the navel. The location of the Tanjon is closest to CV6 of the meridian points in acupuncture.

Chih-I (Zhiyi, 538–597 CE), the founder of T'ien-T'ai (Tiantai) school in Buddhism, in his brilliant work *Mohe Zhiguan (Mo-ho chih-kuan,* 摩訶止観 in Chinese) systemizing the Buddhist teachings, described the Tanjon technique as a technique borrowed from Taoism and pointed out the health benefits of the Tanjon practice (T'ien-T'ai, Chih-I, 1911, p. 108a; see also Chih-I, 1997).

The Founding Head Dharma Master of Won Buddhism, Sot'aesan, explained the benefits of the Tanjon approach in "IV. The Necessity of Concentrating at Elixir Field (Tanjon)" in "Chapter Four: Sitting in Meditation" under "Part Three: Practice" of *The Canon* (Chung, 2003, p.147):

*It is a common practice since ancient times that sitting in meditation, one is to eliminate all thoughts by concentrating one's mind on the unitary mental sphere. Thus, there are various methods of concentration in accordance with each advocacy and expedient; however, if the mind is concentrated on the head or an external mental sphere, thoughts are stirred and the fiery energy ascends, making it difficult to calm the mind. If, however, the mind is concentrated at the elixir field (tanjon), thoughts are not easily stirred and the fiery energy descends, making it easy to calm the mind.*

Sot'aesan himself indicates two beneficial aspects of the Tanjon approach in meditation. One of them is health maintenance, which is not separate from spiritual awakening (Ibid., p. 147):

*Concentration at the elixir field is not only necessary for sitting in meditation; it is of vital importance to the preservation of health.[5] If one concentrates one's mind on the elixir field and swallows the water (saliva) springing from the jade-pond (salivary duct) plentifully, the watery and fiery energies will be balanced and suffering from physical illness will diminish. One's complexion will become lustrous; one's vital force will be replete and one will attain to the mental decoction (simmdan) that secures longevity. Thus, the concentration at the elixir field serves two purposes, the calmness of Zen (sonjong)[6] and health.*

The Taoist principle of water arising and fire descending adopted by Sot'aesan will later be discussed in the section concerning meditation methods. For now, we just want to explain the second important motive behind Sot'aesan's choice of the Tanjon meditation technique, namely, his view that the separation of meditation time and study is the most productive way for the majority of people to attain Buddhahood (Ibid., pp. 147–148):

*The advocates of kanhwa-Son[7] denounce the concentration at the elixir field, alleging that the practice leads one to a dead meditation of senselessness. Kanhwa-Son, however, can be adopted as a provisional expedient only for certain people; it cannot be practiced by the general public. If one concentrates on hwadu for a long time, one can easily become ill because of the rush of blood to the head. Furthermore, those who cannot by nature become caught up in hwadu will lose interest in meditation.*

*Therefore, we set the time for sitting in meditation and the time for the inquiry into hwadu separately so that one can devote oneself to one of them at a time. In this way the perfect calmness and wisdom can both be brought to completion. In this way one can be safeguarded against losing oneself in emptiness and calmness and against exhausting mental discriminations. In this way, one can attain to the essence of True Thusness devoid of motion and rest.*

The quotations above, as one can see, are related to the Won Buddhist reformation approach of making meditation more accessible to the vast lay majority.

# CHAPTER 4
# THE METHOD OF SITTING IN MEDITATION

Before we discuss the methods, we would like to remind the reader that after his enlightenment, "Sot'aesan surveyed the *Four Classics* and the *Hsiao-ching (Filial Piety)* of Confucianism; the *Chin-kang ching (Diamond Sutra)*, the *Sonyo (Essentials of Zen)*, the *Pulgyo taejon (Compendium of Buddhism)*, and the *P'alsangjon (Eight Aspects of the Buddha's Life)* of Buddhism; the *Yin-fu ching (Secret Planning)* and *Yu-shu ching (Jade Hinge)* of Taoism; *the Tonggyong taejon (Compendium of Eastern Learning)* and the *Kasa (Hymns)* of *Ch'ondogyo*; and the *Old and New Testaments of Christianity*" (Scripture of Sot'aesan, *Taejonggyong*, in Chung, 2003, p. 167). Thus, some of the sources for and comments on the meditation instructions are obvious. Others are less so, especially when their elements are present in various traditions, and sometimes, it may not even be possible to determine exactly from which source Won Buddhism inherited a given method.

Now, we take a closer look into the methods, point by point, supplying each of them with some comments. To mark the points under consideration throughout the text, we will place them in square brackets as below:

*[1. Sit on a mat comfortably; hold your head and back straight in an upright, seated posture...]*

The source of this part of Won Buddhism instruction may be traced to shamanistic and Yoga practices lost in time in the ages before Buddha. This part is shared by various traditions of meditation. However, we would not be mistaken too much if we assume that Sot'aesan, in his instruction for meditation, in many aspects was paying tribute directly to *Zazen* of Japanese Zen master Dōgen Kigen (1200-1253). In turn, Dōgen's instruction sources can be traced back to *Mohe Zhiguan*, by Chih-I. Dōgen's Zazen instruction was definitely known to Sot'aesan, and it says (Dumoulin, 1990, p. 75), "*To sit properly, first lay down a thick pillow and on the top of this a second (round) one.*"

The use of a sitting mat, as the Venerable Chwasan (Yi, Kwang Jung, born 1936) the Fourth Head Dharma Master of Won Buddhism, explains in his comments on the Instruction for Meditation in Won Buddhism (2006, pp. 15-16):

> ...*is necessary to prevent pain during sitting meditation. [...] The merit of sitting meditation does not result instantly but requires considerable time as it disciplines and tames our spirit. When one sits for a long time, the buttocks are overstrained, which can easily lead to physical pain.*

To avoid the pain, thus, we need a mat, though the sitting mat is not necessary or directly related to Zen.

Since the Fourth Head Dharma Master's comments are important for understanding the official view on meditation in Won Buddhism, we will henceforth use his opinion often.

In Bongkil Chung's translation of the *Instruction*, the cross-legged position is discussed in detail only in a footnote, whereas the translation by Pal Khn Chon (1988, p. 47) directly reads as follows: "*Sit on a cushion in a relaxed posture with the legs folded. Keep the head erect and the back straight.*"

Let us see now what Dōgen's instruction reads on the subject (Dumoulin, 1990, p.75): "*One may sit either in the full or half cross-legged position. In the full position one places the right foot on the left thigh and the left foot on the right thigh. In the half position, only the left foot is placed upon the right thigh.*"

Now compare that with the Ven. Chwasan comments on the issue in Won Buddhism (Chwasan, 2006, pp. 16-17):

> *This is the method of sitting with the legs crossed: the seated posture with one leg placed on the other. [...] The cross-legged posture enables one to endure for the longest time with head and back erect. The center of gravity is uniformly distributed onto the buttocks and the legs so that one can sit very comfortably for a long time. For beginners, seating in the cross-legged position may not be easy; it can cause pain because the joints have already been stiffened. But when one is accustomed to it, it becomes the most comfortable posture."*

As one can see, whereas in Dōgen's version of the instruction the position of the legs is prescribed and fixed, it is not so in Won Buddhism. Pay attention to the following thoughtful commentary by Chwasan (*Ibid.*, p. 17):

> *if one practices sitting meditation for too long in the half lotus posture without alternating the leg positions, though one may feel very comfortable at*

*first, eventually the pelvis can be twisted, as well as the spinal cord, creating back pain or illness. Thus from the beginning one should alternate one's legs.*

Chwasan also adds a passage about the importance of the spinal cord as the main passageway for the nervous system and the necessity of keeping it straight and unimpaired.

Noteworthy is the fact that the positioning of the hands and the thumbs during meditation is described in detail by Dōgen, whereas in Won Buddhism, we do not see any indication on that issue. The reason for that is not quite clear. Sot'aesan's inattention to the positioning of the hands and the thumbs could be explained either by Sot'aesan's familiarity with several meditation traditions that prescribe mutually exclusive hand mudras, or, even more likely, by the Taoist tradition that left this issue to the practitioner to allow him or her to choose the hand positioning best suited to his or her specific external and internal conditions.

As for an upright posture, the importance of which was stressed by Dōgen, the Won Buddhism teachings follow suit in decreeing that the head and the spine should be aligned (*Ibid.*, p. 12) since *"with even the slightest deviation, one cannot reap the desired benefits of sitting meditation. The back is the first place distortion occurs, which then spreads to the whole body and to the mind."*

In explaining Won meditation, Chwasan once again reminds that the correct posture not only keeps the mind alert but also preserves the spine's health and helps one enter the reality of Zen.

The part on sitting straight can also be found in a variety of earlier instructions. For instance, compare it with the following Taoist text (*Treatise on Sitting Forgetting*, p. 101): *"With external affairs cut off so that there is nothing to get on your mind, then sit straight and gaze inwardly with accurate awareness."*

**[Loosen the tension of the body and gather it at the elixir field (tanjon); be aware only of the physical energy concentrated at the elixir field...]**

The Fourth Head Dharma Master of Won Buddhism comments thus (Chwasan, 2006, p. 21): *"Since ancient times, resting in the Danjeon (Tanjon) has been highly praised as the best technique for meditation purposes as well as for physical health."*

As we already discussed earlier, the practice of resting in the Tanjon came to Korean Buddhism from China along with Taoist and Ch'an

Buddhist practices. Conventionally, the practice is considered to be adopted by Ch'an practitioners from Taoism. We cannot fail to consider, however, that similar practices were widespread in the region and were empirically found at one or another historical point by adepts and followers of different ancient meditation practices.

Chwasan, in his comments on the *Instruction*, further teaches thus (*Ibid.*, 2006, pp. 23-24):

> *one should start the zen of resting in the Danjeon with the state of mind that one brings down the strength of the head, shoulders, and torso, while maintaining an erect posture. Then the Danjeon will be the center of energy that spreads through the whole body; it becomes the sea and source of all energy. It becomes the pillar of all the energy in the body.*

The Tanjon is easily located: it is three fingers (two and a half inches) below and two fingers behind the navel and is the body's center of gravity, but it is not easy to focus there in actual practice, and settling the Tanjon requires quite a long time. To avoid malpractice that may result in pain or a disease, one should follow the proper technique, which should be taught by an experienced teacher. The Tanjon is believed to be a source of physical energy, inner power, and reproductive vitality; it is also connected to the physiological functions of digestion and elimination. Psychologically, it functions by giving us a sense of stability and balance. The negative effects of incorrect practice may result in the imbalance of water and fire energies in the body; the imbalance would manifest itself in abdominal pain, headache, oedema, or other malfunctions produced by the incorrect circulation of water and fire energies. With the wrong Tanjon settling, one may find that energy and tension arise in the body or dissipate during meditation.

We found information about the complications in settling the Tanjon, as well as an extended explanation of the importance of the Tanjon (*hara* in Japanese) as the vital center of man, in the amazing book by K. G. Dürckheim (2004), whose fascinating study is totally devoted just to this single subject. The author explains thus (Dürckheim, 2004, pp.8-9):

> *The Japanese term Hara means nothing other than the physical embodiment of the original Life center in man. Man is originally endowed and invested with Hara. But when, as a rational being, he loses what is embodied in Hara it becomes his task to regain it. To rediscover the unity concealed in contradictions through which he perceives life intellectually is the nerve of his existence.*

> ...Hara is that state in which the individual has found his primal center, and has proven himself by it. When we speak of the state of an individual we mean something that concerns him in his entirety, that is, something that transcends the duality of body and soul.

In representations of the Buddha—in Buddha statues, for example—we find an emphasis on the center time and again. Regardless of whether the Buddha is sitting in meditation or standing with his hands raised to the sky, Buddha statues place the center of gravity in the center of the body. This occurrence is known to be entirely unrelated to the Buddha's corpulence as earlier statues depicting him to be much thinner also show the center of gravity in the lower abdomen.

Analyzing in detail the concept of *hara* in the context of the Japanese culture, Dürckheim makes this conclusion:

> ...the word Hara denotes something that gives the man possessing it special faculties, active as well as passive, i.e., receptive. Hara gives rise to experiences transcending the range of the five senses but which do not necessary coincide with those arising from instinct or intuition. "Hara" means that entire receptive and creative organ which fundamentally is the "whole man" – able to prove himself as a such. [...] [T]he Hara–practice lifts a man out of prison of his little ego and frees him to live and act from his state of wholeness (Ibid., p. 42).

It is necessary to present here one more extended quote from the study by Durckheim, the quote that is most directly related to our subject of meditation:

> For the Japanese, Hara suwatte imasu, that is the "sedate belly," implies not only a corresponding imperturbability of the heart, an indestructible composure and a state of relaxation but implies also a swift and certain striking power. The imperturbability characterizing the sedate man implies the steadiness of a tranquil mind prepared for anything. He is able to react appropriately in any situation and nothing throws him off balance.
>
> Sitting, which is both outwardly and inwardly correct, is possible only with Hara. Thus, hara ga suwatte imasu, the hara-seat, not only refers to the position and weight of the belly within the whole body but also suggests the whole mood of stable sitting. This stability implies at once an outward and an inward balance... (Ibid., p. 45).

### *[...with no thought dwelling anywhere.]*

If the mind is attached to anything, thoughts will easily dwell on it. The mind then plays with idle and delusive thoughts and loses concentration. It is interesting to note here the similarities and differences in working with the thoughts in Buddhism and Taoism. In Taoism, we can find basically the same requirement for maintaining concentration: "Do not dwell on any thing and the mind will be stable" (*Treatise on Sitting Forgetting*, p. 101).

However, whereas in Buddhism, the recurrence of delusive thoughts should not be considered by a practitioner as annoying or negative but rather helping to advance one's practice, in some Taoist texts, the view is quite the opposite, as, for example, in *Treatise on Sitting Forgetting* ( p. 101):

*As soon as you notice a thought arise, immediately extinguish it; arrest thoughts as they arise, in order to make your mind peaceful and quiet.*

*Next, even though you may not obviously have any obsessions, still floating, wandering, random thoughts are also to be extinguished.*

For sake of correctness, however, we should mention that the interpenetration and mutual influence of Buddhism and Taoism was a norm. Because of that, some late Taoist texts praise and use the Buddhist methods, directly pointing out their Ch'an origin (*Anthology on the Cultivation of Realization*, p. 18.): "*Don't worry about the occurrence of thoughts, only beware of being slow to notice it happening. The occurrence of thought is sickness; not continuing thoughts is medicine.*"

And even more (*Ibid.*, pp. 29-30):

*Mind really does not move; when you reach this point in observing mind, those thoughts cease of themselves.*

*Stopping thoughts is not hard – if you can turn back to before a single thought has arisen, then the preceding thought will naturally not continue.*

*[...] if you want to understand the non-occurrence of a single thought right now, you must examine where thoughts come from. The past is based on the present, the future is based on the past; if you have no mind in the present, the past is naturally over.*

Compare also with the following strikingly Mahayanistic Buddhist passage from the Taoist treatise (*Ibid.*, pp. 29-30):

*There is nothing in the world but one mind. Stirring thoughts create all objects. If thoughts are not produced, objects are spontaneously gone. When you thoroughly examine stirring thoughts, thoughts too are empty and silent. So we know there is nothing lost when deluded and nothing gained when enlightened, because the true mind not dwelling on anything neither increases nor decreases.*

*If your mind is unguarded, the energy loses concentration. If that happens, do not forget to check the concentration of energy.*

The problem of resting in the Tanjon is keeping the mind tamed and concentrated there. In Won sitting meditation, the mind is considered primary and the energy secondary. If energy wanders in all directions, it means that the mind is yet not tamed. The mind is not under control, and it is attached to thoughts, feelings, and desires. Meditation is the way to restore concentration and the original, nondistracted, nonattached mind. In this state, the water and fire energies are in perfect balance. The Fourth Won Buddhism Head Dharma Master reminds us thus (Chwasan, 2006, p. 39): "*…it is the most urgent and necessary thing for practitioners to become accustomed to resting in the Danjeon by whatever means possible.*"

### [3. Keep your breathing uniform, inhaling a little longer and stronger than exhaling.]

Generally speaking, attention to breathing is the aspect that unites practitioners of all meditative practices, even though different practices may require their adepts to perform seemingly quite opposite actions when dealing with breathing.

Since Buddhism came to Korea in its Chinese version and, as a such, it was first of all the Ch'an version of the Buddhist teachings, the influences from Taoism are numerous, undeniable, and obvious.

In Won Buddhism, comments on breathing explain the Taoist view that the breathing should be balanced to the utmost and that the balance should be reached when inhalations are a little longer and stronger and exhalations are a little shorter and weaker. However, mistakenly inhaling much longer and stronger may produce excessive fire energy and lead to the so-called *Zen illness*. If one finds himself or herself in such a situation, he or she should ask for advice from a more advanced practitioner. If the illness reaches a high level, it may prevent a practitioner from further progress in sitting meditation and disconnect him or her from meditation entirely. In this case, it might be necessary to stop sitting meditation and switch to other forms of practice, such as, walking meditation, reciting the name of the Buddha, etc., until the illness vanishes by itself.

The best way to deal with breathing is to unite the focus on the Tanjon with breathing as early as possible. It is not an easy task since observing the breathing may distract a novice from resting in the Tanjon and *vice versa*. To accomplish unity, Chwasan (*Cited*, pp. 42-43) recommends thus:

> *He or she should inhale and exhale through the Danjeon. One should settle the energy in the Danjeon through breathing. If these two coincide simultaneously, no problem arises; breathing helps gather energy in the Danjeon, and the gathering of energy in Danjeon helps breathing. Thus one develops one's power of concentration in regard to this complex matter, and one can be more easily absorbed in the authentic realm of Zen. [...]*
>
> *Finally one will enter the stage in which one does not feel the distinction between inhaling and exhaling, and one is finally absorbed in resting in danjeon. This is a very crucial point.*

Now, compare the Won explanations just cited with the following Taoist passage from *Secret Writings on the mechanisms of Nature* (p. 115):

> *When the mind rests below the navel, that is called womb breathing. Mind and breath submerge together into the region below the navel; keeping them clear and pure naturally is called "not forgetting," while going along with their clarity and purity naturally is called "not fostering".*
> *[...] gradually mind and breath come to stay together, spirit and energy merge harmoniously.*

**[4. To keep the demon of drowsiness away, keep your eyes open; however, you may try with your eyes closed if you feel refreshed as long as there is no danger of drowsiness.]**

Dōgen's Zazen instruction says that "*the eyes should always be open*" (Dumoulin, 1990, p. 76). The problem of drowsiness in meditation is very common. The use of a smacking stick in Zen tradition attests well to this fact. Thus, the instruction in Won Buddhism is very clear: the eyes must be open to prevent sleepiness and drowsiness. Sleepiness is often considered even more harmful than delusive thoughts in meditation because delusive thoughts can at least be noticed by the practitioner. The danger of drowsiness is that it comes unnoticed. Thus, one should practice meditation with his or her eyes open from the beginning. Only after gaining considerable skill in meditation may he or she try sitting with his or her eyes closed.

The Fourth Won Buddhism Head Dharma Master comments thus (Chwasan, 2006, pp. 49-50):

*If one forms a habit of practicing Zen with the eyes closed and dozing off, unlearning that habit is an extremely difficult job. Such a habit cannot be corrected without strong determination and help from others. This cannot be treated lightly, for one cannot be corrected like this all one's life. What a pity that would be!*

*So when one can make a judgment that one will not be affected by drowsiness, one may practice Zen without opening the eyes. However, if there appears some indication of falling into drowsiness, one should immediately open the eyes and not be grasped by drowsiness.*

As we see, Won Buddhism meditation tradition recommends closing the eyes only with strong precautions and extreme awareness, whereas the Taoist treatise *Taiji Alchemy Secrets*, for instance, instructs one to do quite the opposite (p. 120): "*Sit down, close your eyes, become aware of the spirit, quiet the mind, and tune the breathing.*"

We suppose that the Head Dharma Master Sot'aesan's stipulation that the eyes should be open was based not only on his preference for Buddhism over other teachings but also—and even more so—on practical considerations. As we discussed earlier, Sot'aesan's lifetime goal was to bring Buddhism to the general public, and he knew very well the hardships of people who worked long hours to make ends meet. Sitting still even for a moment with their eyes closed would certainly induce sleepiness and drowsiness in most of Sot'aesan's followers, who were hardworking simple peasants and workers.

### [5. Keep your mouth always closed.]

The Fourth Head Dharma Master of Won Buddhism explains this passage in terms of energy circulation from a position not different from a Taoist view (Chwasan, 2006, pp. 51-52):

*It is a well-known fact that in daily life when one stiffens one's resolution, one becomes taut and one's mouth becomes firmly closed; this is a natural phenomenon. When one is completely attentive, and one's energy is centered, one can gather and direct one's energy at will. But when one's resolution flags, the closed mouth is apt to loosen.*

*We can stay alert without one moment of being inattentive by keeping the mouth resolutely closed. In this frame of mind, one collects the energy that is dispersed, and one can enter the authentic realm of absorption in accord with the energy and mind.*

**[If the ascent of the watery energy and the descent of the fiery energy go well as the practice matures, clear and smooth saliva will flow from the salivary gland, which you may gather in the mouth and swallow once in a while.]**

This position is of special interest because of its obvious Taoist origin. In Taoism, all energies are in permanent interaction, and the energy of the human body is in communion with heaven and earth (*Anthology on the Cultivation of Realization*, p. 11): "I have read that the Sun going down into the Earth is a symbol of the fire of the heart descending, and the moon reaching the center of the sky is a symbol of the water of the kidneys rising."

Countless passages on the issue are found in Taoist sources, for instance, in *Secret Writings on the Mechanisms of Nature* (p. 115):

> *Bai Yuzhan said, "the path of inner refinement is extremely simple and easy; just get the fire of the heart to descend into the elixir field. The elixir field is the chamber of water, while the heart is fire. When fire enters water, then water and fire mix and true yang is produced.*
>
> *Master Wang Chongyang said, "... Alternating Exhalation and inhalation come and go in the furnace of creation; after a long time this becomes thoroughly familiar, and fire will naturally erupt from below the navel, a tiger will emerge from the water. Without even trying to return to central balance, you spontaneously revert to central balance.*

In Taoist tradition, after a certain period, concentration on the Tanjon increasingly produces energy (*Taiji Alchemy Secrets*, p. 119): "Water and fire naturally commingle, and heaven and earth join."

The practice belongs to the practices of inner alchemy and is called "spirit produces energy and energy produces spirit."

Opposition Fire-Water is one of the fundamental dualities of Yin-Yang in Taoism and Chinese medicine. Dr. Maciocia, in his book *The Foundations of Chinese Medicine* (2005, pp. 11–12) explains thus:

> *The balance between Fire and Water in the body is crucial. Fire is essential to all physiological processes: it represents the flame that keeps alive and stokes all metabolic processes. Fire, the physiological Fire, assists the Heart in its function of housing the Mind (Shen), it provides the warmth necessary to the Spleen to transform and transport, it stimulates the Small Intestine*

*functions of separation, it provides the heat necessary to the Bladder and Lower Burner to transform and excrete fluids and it provides the heat necessary for the Uterus to keep the Blood moving.*

*If the physiological Fire declines, the Mind will suffer with depression, the Spleen cannot transform and transport, the Small Intestine cannot separate the fluids, the Bladder and Lower Burner cannot excrete the fluids and there will be oedema, and the Uterus turns Cold, which may cause infertility.*

*This physiological Fire is called the Fire of the Gate of Life (Ming Men) and derives from the Kidneys.*

*Water has the function of moistening and cooling during all the body's physiological functions, to balance the warming action of the physiological Fire. The origin of Water is also from the kidneys.*

*Thus, the balance between Fire and Water is fundamental to all physiological processes of the body. Fire and Water balance and keep a check on each other in every single physiological process. When Fire gets out of hand and becomes excessive, it has a tendency to flow upwards, hence the manifestations will show on the top part of the body and head, with headaches, red eyes, red face or thirst. When Water becomes excessive, it has a tendency to flow downwards causing oedema of the legs, excessive urination or incontinence.*

Fire is Yang in nature and corresponds to movement; Water is Yin in nature and corresponds to stillness. Fire and Water must be in balance in the body since they represent the two fundamental poles, Yang and Yin. Maciocia continues to explain on their interrelationship (*Ibid.*, p. 174):

*It should be stressed here that although from a Five-Element perspective Fire and Water control each other (i.e. Fire dries up Water and Water douses Fire), in this context Fire and Water interact with each other and mutually nourish each other. The relationship between Fire and Water highlights the importance of a connection and link between these two Elements and therefore between Heart and Kidneys. [...] Heart-Qi descends to the Kidneys, which hold it; likewise, Kidney-Qi ascends to the Heart.*

*Heart-Yang descends to warm Kidney-Yin; Kidney-Yin ascends to nourish and cool Heart-Yang. The energy of the Heart and Kidneys is in constant interchange above and below. Chinese medicine refers to this as the 'mutual support of Fire and Water', or the 'mutual support of Heart and Kidneys.'*

In Chinese medicine, thus, when Taoist functions are applied to body functions and physiology, Fire and Water assist each other.

The Won Buddhism instructions for meditation pay close attention to and are in complete accordance with the idea that the human body operates through the harmony of water and fire.

The Taoist view on the circulation of water and fire energies in the body was praised and cherished by Sot'aesan; it is explained, for instance, in his scripture in the following passage (Scripture of Sot'aesan, *Taejonggyong 3.15*, in Chung, 2003, p. 202):

> 15. *One of his disciples asked about the ascending watery energy and the descending fiery energy, and the master answered, "water by its nature is cool and clear and has the tendency to descend, while fire by its nature is hot and turbid and has the tendency to ascend. When you are involved in a complicated thought, you feel a rush of blood to the head. When this happens, the sap of life gets dried up and your head feels hot and your spirit becomes turbid. This is because the fiery energy ascends and the watery energy descends. If your mind is cleared of the complicated thought and the vital force is calmed down, your head feels cool and your spirit becomes clear with clear saliva circulating in the mouth. This is because the watery energy ascends and the fiery energy descends.*

As for saliva, in Taoist techniques of inner alchemy, swallowing saliva is so important that it is a part of all exercises, coming usually at the beginning and the end of each stage of an exercise. Saliva accomplishes two complementary functions in Taoist practices. The first is the rinsing of the mouth, which is a purifying function. The *Wai-Ching* (Robinet, 1993, p. 90) refers to this technique when it advises a person to purify the mouth (the flowery lake).

In Taoism, however, the more essential function of saliva seems to be the nourishment of immortality during the course of meditation, as it was described in the *Ch'u-tz'u* (compare this to Sot'aesan's scripture, according to which, saliva should be swallowed to benefit the practitioner's health). The *Wai-Ching* says that "*one who is thirsty can obtain the liquor and the one who is famished can satisfy himself,*" and the commentary on this passage says that it is the *ch'i* that satisfies hunger and the saliva that quenches thirst. Throughout the *Huang-t'ing Ching*, saliva is treated as the water of life. The text on breathing technique compares saliva to a beneficent rain that soaks the earth—it "*swallows up dryness.*" Whereas breathing "*makes the clouds advance,*" swallowing saliva is concerned with "spreading the rain."

The *Ta-tung chen-ching* follows the tradition and says that swallowing saliva brings life to the hundred thousand spirits. As it says, the "*divine water of the flowery lake flows and gushes out to irrigate and moisten the body"* (*Ibid.*, p. 91).

The scripture on the Nourishment of the Vital Principle and the Prolongation of Life, which is attributed to T'ao Hung-ching, also states that the saliva irrigates the body and transforms and nourishes the hundred thousand spirits. Because of this, the members, joints, bodily hair, and hair on the head are firm and solid, and one enjoys an eternal springtime. This is why saliva is called the "golden beverage" (*chin-chiang*), and one must not let saliva leave the body or be expectorated; rather, he or she must always swallow and preserve it.

In the *Huang-t'ing Ching*, saliva is seen as a precious nectar that is given diverse names. It is variously called "divine juice" (*ling-i*), "gold liqueur" (*chin-li*), and "pure water of the jade lake" (*yu-tz'u ch'ing-shui*). It is also referred to as the "mysterious source" (*hsuan-chuan*). Moreover, if we believe the commentators, saliva is given still other qualifying names, such as "jade juice" (*yu-i*), "sweet source" (*li-ch'uan*), "source of jade" (*yu-ch'uan*), "jade sap" (*yu-chin*), and "jade beverage" (*yu-chiang*). In Taoist texts it is ordinarily called the "jade juice," an expression anciently used in the *Ch'u-tz'u* (in the poem titled "Yuan-ch'i") for divine food (jade, it may be noted, is the Yin part of the couple jade-gold; *ibid.*, p. 91).

All the Taoist connotations above were known to Sot'aesan. When talking about saliva, Sot'aesan used exactly the same epithets that appear in Taoist texts, such as "clear and smooth saliva." However, the elaborate Taoist conceptions about and practices with saliva were reduced by Sot'aesan to the practical points understandable to and useful for a lay practitioner.

**[6. Let your spirit be wakeful in calmness and calm in wakefulness; if you become drowsy, collect your mind to freshen the spirit; if your mind turns to delusive thoughts, replace them with right thought; then stay in the realm of the True Thusness of your original nature.]**

Since ancient times, to be wakeful in calmness and calm in wakefulness is considered the true standard for the practitioners of meditation. This requirement means to be tranquil with a clear mind and to be calm in alertness. In the Taoist treatise *The Anthology on the Cultivation of Realization* (p. 78), it is explained in terms of its necessity for balance:

*The ancient sage Yao said, "Hold sincerely to this balance." Holding to balance refers to both action and quiet. When you are quiet, you hold to this balance by conscious presence of mind. When you are active, you hold to this balance by adapting to events. "Sincerely" means trusting; it has the sense of spontaneously keeping balance at all times, whatever happens, without the slightest effort or interruption.*

Note this last sentence about effortless spontaneity because we will soon return to that concept.

The Fourth Head Dharma Master of Won Buddhism explains thus (Chwasan, 2006, p.59):

*Ultimately, there is no distinction between being ever calm in alertness and being ever alert in calmness, but only the state of being steadfastly settled in the genuine realm of Samādhi. In this orientation, sitting meditation is not trapped in mere alertness and does not fall into torpid calmness, but enters into the true Samādhi of our original nature.*

When we are calm, it is easy to lapse into sleepiness; and when we stay alert, many idle and delusive thoughts may distract our mind. To avoid both wrong sides, Master Sot'aesan instructed that a practitioner fight torpor and drowsiness by refreshing his or her spirit and get rid of wandering thoughts with right mindfulness.

Falling into sleepiness and drowsiness and not being aware of it may bring a practitioner into an even deeper torpor from which it is even more difficult to surface. It is better to not allow oneself to become sleepy from the beginning and correct the situation immediately when it is noticed.

As for right mindfulness, it is said thus (*Ibid.*, pp. 61-62):

*The only right mental activity while in sitting meditation is being aware only of the meditation. Everything else is just an idle, irrelevant, and disturbing function of the mind. Hence, to restore it with right mindfulness is to revive one-pointedness in your mind."*

*It is imperative that you resolutely restore your spirit to right mindfulness and rest in danjeon. Under no circumstances should you fail to do so.*

**[...then stay in the realm of the True Thusness of your original nature.]**

The ultimate goal of sitting meditation is staying in the realm of Buddha nature. This state is naturally pure and devoid of everything. This state of original nature is difficult to understand since when a person enters it, all mental fabrications cease; there are no thoughts, no knowledge, no anything. This is the most enjoyable state, effortless and spontaneous. It is interesting to note that Chwasan, in his commentaries, uses the English translation in which there is an addition not found in several other translations of *The Canon*. This addition is the characterization of the original nature (the original face) as "effortless and spontaneous" (Chwasan, 2006, p. 63).

And now, it is time to recollect the passage from the Taoist *Anthology on the Cultivation of Realization* cited earlier. Without detailed manuscript studies, it is not possible to determine whether the origin of this description was of Taoist or Buddhist descent. The two systems of thought so strongly influenced each other that even prominent scholars are at times unable to distinguish between the two with regard to some aspects.

Chwasan explains that "effortless" means no doing and no thinking and warns that this effortless state is often misconceived by inexperienced people as a state without purpose or reason. He warns that one must differentiate the true void from the false void (Chwasan, 2006, pp. 63-64):

> *The true void refers to the realm in which pure and clear life force is at its peak, attainable through repeated filtering out of impurities. The false void refers to a state void of pure and clear life force, resulting from the repeated accumulation of impurities that have not been filtered out. It is crucial to overcome the false void of resting in calmness without right mindfulness. If a practitioner falls into this false void, irrevocable misfortune will result. This is where the so-called dark hell starts to sprout.*

The next three points in the instructions for meditation in Won Buddhism are dedicated to the things to beware:

**[7. The beginner at sitting in meditation sometimes suffers from pain in the legs and the invasion of delusive thoughts. If your legs ache, you may change their positions, one upon the other. If delusive thoughts invade your mind, recognize them only as delusive thoughts; then they will disappear of themselves. Do not be vexed with or discouraged by them.]**

The simplicity in Won Buddhism's approach to practical aspects of meditation is amazing. The instructions do not go into complicated Indian symbolism, like "the Buddha's sitting posture with legs crossed and soles upward, left over right being the attitude for subduing demons, right over left for blessing, the hands being placed one above the other in similar order." Instead, in accordance with Sot'aesan's aim to bring Buddhism to the broad public, recommendations are simple, clear, and down-to-earth. His successor's commentary on this passage is of the same order of clarity (Chwasan, 2006, pp. 65-66): *"Aching legs prove that your body is alive and the invasion by idle thoughts proves that your spirit is alive. [...] It is only natural, not strange, that your legs ache and idle thoughts bother your mind."*

Switching the position of the legs is no problem. That is a profound difference from the rigid requirements of some other schools. Everything should be reasonably considered, and depending on a person's conditions, the legs' position can be switched. However, in some translations, there is an important word there, *occasionally*. The course of meditation should not be interrupted, neither by unnecessary attempts to endure the pain of aching legs nor by constant distracting movements.

As for delusive thoughts, it is written that during meditation, any thought, correct or incorrect, necessary or unnecessary—any thought that interferes with single-mindedness—is delusive. And the nature of delusive thoughts is such that they retreat from those who are not discouraged or vexed by their presence but simply recognize them as delusive.

**[8. If you sit in meditation for the first time, your face and body may feel itchy occasionally as if ants were crawling over them. Be sure not to touch or scratch. This is the symptom of the blood passing through the blood vessels.]**

There are several common phenomena experienced by virtually all practitioners of meditation. Whereas in other branches of Buddhism or in other meditation practices, those issues are not always directly addressed in the main texts or scriptures, Sot'aesan was attentive to the important issues of daily practice, rightly assuming that explaining these issues is absolutely necessary to support the practice of meditation by novices and for their spiritual growth.

Chwasan's comments on the eighth passage of the instruction is that sitting meditation promotes more active blood flow through the capillaries, which causes itching that should be ignored since it soon ends by itself in a healthy person (Chwasan, 2006, p. 77). Chwasan's comments contradict neither modern nor traditional medicine, and his explanation likely does not contradict any explanation that Sot'aesan himself gave.

*[9. While sitting in meditation, do not search for any extraordinary pivotal point or any miraculous traces; should you notice such phenomena, recognize them as wicked and pass over them as nothing worthy of attention.]*

The Taoist treatise *Anthology on the Cultivation of Realization* also warns us (pp. 70–71) against mysterious manifestations:

*When beginning to cultivate stabilization, one may suddenly awaken psychic powers, such as knowledge of the past, knowledge of the future, knowledge of other's minds, or uninhibited eloquence. That is what Confucians call the Way of perfect truthfulness, by which foreknowledge is possible.*

*When they learn this much of the Way, many people crave wordly fame, profit, and honor. All this belongs to contaminated spirit and energy; since it cannot be assured, many take to voluntary disembodiment. This should be immediately abandoned, because contaminated phenomena are not real.*

The Won Buddhism teachings interpret any occurrences of the mysterious phenomena referenced above in a similar way. Sot'aesan warns strongly against mysticism and seeking extraordinary abilities. Supernatural occurrences may take various forms, and people experiencing them often mistake them as an achievement of great spiritual power. However, in reality, they are dangerous delusions that end in misfortune and suffering for many. In his comments on this passage, Chwasan is entirely strict (2006, p. 79):

*Occurences such as these have no relevance to the principle of our original nature. They have nothing whatsoever to do with awakening the principles of the great and the small, being and nonbeing, or the principle of cause and effect. Nor do they have any connection to understanding right and wrong, or benefit and harm. Hence, they have no relevance to the deliverance of our souls or the attainment of our spiritual freedom. They do not provide any kind of help.*

Chwasan explains that Sot'aesan's instruction to pay mysterious manifestations no attention means that one must not cling to such phenomena yet must, at the same time, not think that they are something bad (*Ibid.*). If treated unconcernedly, lightly, and without either liking or affliction, they will be powerless and disappear by themselves. Very close attention should be paid to this matter.

*[If you practice sitting in meditation for a long time as described above, you will eventually forget the distinction between subject and object, time and place, remaining in the realm of the True Thusness of your original nature and rejoicing in unparalleled spiritual bliss.]*

Compare with the final words of instruction for meditation in Dōgen's treatise entitled *Fukanzazengi* (Dumoulin, 1990, p. 76.): "*If you practice in this way for a long time, you will forget all attachments and concentration will come naturally. That is the art of Zazen. Zazen is the Dharma gate of great rest and joy.*"

# CHAPTER 5
# THE BENEFITS OF MEDITATION:
## WON BUDDHISM INSTRUCTIONS AND CONTEMPORARY STUDIES ON MEDITATION

It would be useful to start this chapter with a detailed description of the merits of the practice of meditation as it was understood by Sot'aesan (Chung, 2003, pp. 144–145):

*III. The Merits*
*If one attains the power of sitting in meditation after a long period of practice, one will reap the following ten benefits.*
*1. Rash and thoughtless behavior gradually diminish.*
*2. The operation of the six sense organs becomes orderly.*
*3. Suffering from illness diminishes and one's complexion brightens up.*
*4. One's memory improves.*
*5. One's patience grows.*
*6. Attachment lessens.*
*7. Vicious dispositions change into right ones.*
*8. The wisdom of one's original nature shines.*
*9. One will enjoy supreme bliss.*
*10. One will gain liberty from birth and death.*

Setting apart some of the chapter points that cannot be proved (yet?) by modern scientific methods, we want to demonstrate here the correlation of the merits listed in Won Buddhism instructions with the recent findings in research on meditation. Recently, there have been numerous studies of the different aspects of meditation. Although those studies were not conducted in Won Buddhism meditation per se, they cover various meditation types and methods, and such studies are often performed at the frontiers of modern knowledge by using cutting-edge technologies unavailable just a decade ago.

First, we shall discuss brain research. A detailed synopsis of the current state of research on the effects of meditation on the brain can be found in *Zen-Brain Reflections*, by James H. Austin (2006). A clinical neurologist and researcher, Dr. Austin, an experienced meditator himself, composed a book on the different aspects of recent research in meditation, including a research involving electroencephalography (EEG), magnetic resonance imaging (MRI), neurochemistry, etc. Answering the question "What is the most striking practical benefit you attributed to Zen practice?" he wrote, "*One discovers a sense of increasing calmness and clarity while beginning to walk the Zen meditative Path. This evolves over the years, because the practice points one increasingly in the direction of simplicity, stability, efficient action, and compassion*" (Ibid., p. xxvi; italics mine).

To help patients cope with stress, pain, and illness by using the mindfulness practice of moment-to-moment awareness, Dr. Jon Kabat-Zinn created the Mindfulness-Based Stress Reduction (MBSR) program on the basis of Buddhist meditation and Yoga, and in 1979, he began teaching it at the Stress Reduction Clinic in Worcester, Massachusetts. The program demonstrated itself to be highly effective, and Kabat-Zinn has made significant contributions to modern science with his research that focuses on the use of mind-body interactions for healing and on the various clinical applications of mindfulness meditation training for people with chronic pain, cancer, and heart and/or stress-related disorders.

Newberg et al. (2010) demonstrated through SPECT imaging the cerebral blood flow (CBF) differences between long-term meditators and nonmeditators. The CBF of long-term meditators was significantly higher ($p<0.05$) compared to nonmeditators in the prefrontal cortex, parietal cortex, thalamus, putamen, caudate, and midbrain. There was also a significant difference in the thalamic laterality with long-term meditators having greater asymmetry. Physical evidence of the observed changes associated with long-term meditation appears in both the brain structures that underlie the attention network and those that relate to emotion and autonomic function.

Zeidan et al. (2010) demonstrated recently that not only long-term but even short-term mindfulness meditation practice promotes executive functioning and the ability to sustain attention. Brief meditation training was also found to reduce fatigue and anxiety and increase mindfulness. Moreover, brief mindfulness training significantly improved visuospatial processing, working memory, and executive functioning. The findings suggest that four days of meditation training can enhance the ability to sustain attention, benefits that have previously been reported with long-term meditators.

Himelstein (2010) presents evidence that meditation-based programs can help rehabilitate incarcerated populations. Overall, research suggests three areas in which meditation-based programs provide appreciable results in criminal offenders: enhancement of psychological well-being, a decrease in substance use, and a decrease in recidivism. This suggests that meditation-based programs may be appropriate for use in the rehabilitation for populations in correctional institutions.

Rosenzweig et al. (2010) compared changes in bodily pain, health-related quality of life (HRQoL), and psychological symptoms during an eight-week Mindfulness-Based Stress Reduction program among groups of participants with different chronic pain conditions. They concluded that the effects of MBSR treatment on pain, health-related quality of life, and psychological well-being vary as a function of chronic pain condition and compliance to the recommended home meditation practice. Participants with arthritis showed the largest benefit from MBSR treatment for health-related quality of life and psychological distress.

Creswell et al. (2009) studied the effects of an eight-week MBSR program on biological markers of HIV-1 progression, namely, on $CD4^+$ T lymphocyte counts in stressed HIV-infected adults. This study provides an initial indication that mindfulness meditation training can slow the decline of $CD4^+$ T lymphocyte levels in HIV-1 infected-adults.

Witek-Janusek et al. (2008) evaluated the effect of an MBSR program on immune function, quality of life (QOL), and coping in women recently diagnosed with breast cancer. Their study found that women enrolled in the MBSR program had reduced cortisol levels, improved QOL, and increased coping effectiveness compared to the non-MBSR group. The study concluded that MBSR program can be of help to women recently diagnosed with an early-stage breast cancer, and the results provide preliminary evidence that MSBR benefits immune function, QOL, and coping.

Sudsuang et al. (1991) reported that after meditation, serum cortisol levels were significantly reduced, serum total protein level was significantly increased, and systolic pressure, diastolic pressure, and pulse rate were all significantly reduced. Vital capacity, tidal volume, and maximal voluntary ventilation were significantly lower after meditation. There were also significant decreases in reaction time after mediation practice. The percentage decrease in reaction time during meditation was 22 percent, while in subjects untrained in meditation, the percentage decrease was only 7 percent. These results indicate that practicing Dhammakāya Buddhist meditation produces biochemical and physiological changes and reduces one's reaction time.

Zen meditation practice could protect a person from cognitive decline usually associated with age and enhance antioxidant activity. From a clinical point of view, Zen meditation was found to reduce stress and blood pressure and be efficacious for a variety of conditions (Chiesa, 2009).

The early research illuminating the mechanisms responsible for the life-span-extending and health-enhancing effects of meditation, visualization, and systematic relaxation points to the importance of their anti-inflammatory, antistress, and antioxidant effects as well as their impact on enhancing the production of endogenous substances that possess general longevity-enhancing, regenerative properties (Olivo, 2009).

We could continue further quoting current studies on meditation; however, even our brief selection of scientific studies is sufficient to demonstrate and confirm the numerous merits of meditation.

For those interested in a more detailed bibliography of meditation studies, we would recommend a book by Murphy M. and Donovan S. (1997) that contains a review of meditation research performed between 1931 and 1996.

As in any scientific field, reviews, revalidation, and translation into practice are endless tasks. There are many unexplored areas in meditation research that could be pursued to expand the scientific understanding of meditation. For instance, it would be interesting to study the influence of meditation on the speed and quality of decision making in situations of high stress, on recognition abilities, on the creative abilities of poets and musicians, and on athletic performance. It would also be interesting to evaluate meditation's effects on long- and short-term memory, treatment of coordination disorders, and blood clotting and its possible applications in childbirth. Yet another possible direction of research could be to compare different meditation techniques side by side using the same parameters of evaluation. The list of suggestions is endless indeed, and the discipline of studying meditation scientifically is currently on the rise.

# Afterword

We want to emphasize that in the twentieth century, Buddhism in Korea was undergoing a conversion from its normative canonical tradition to its modernized versions, including Won Buddhism. The modernization in Won Buddhism was based not only on the original Buddhist thought. To a great deal, it was based on Sot'aesan's personal view of the religion in a specific Korean context. The new Won Buddhism movement began with Sot'aesan interpreting Buddhist scriptures in a personally meaningful and relevant way. In a sense, the personal input he made is unique. He deliberately used the canonical tradition and pursued his own way to propagate a new approach to religion functioning in the modern Korean society. His interpretation was streamlined, controversial issues were omitted or even rejected, and programs of practice were institutionalized, including a fresh approach to sitting meditation.

The basic techniques of sitting meditation, to a great degree, were adopted by the Founding Head Dharma Master Sot'aesan from Taoism. The techniques were creatively incorporated into Buddhist context, with changes appropriate for the Korean society of the time. His choice of meditation practice was made on the basis of a great number of considerations, including his realization of the profoundness of the Buddha's teachings, his unique experience of enlightenment, and the necessity to make Buddhism available to the vast majority of people. His compilation of the instructions for meditation in Won Buddhism was a colossal effort that required the examination and comprehension of a plethora of various religious teachings, as well as a detailed understanding of the needs of laypeople in regard to meditation practice.

Now completed, the instructions for meditation in Won Buddhism, containing the wisdom of generations of meditation practitioners, represent in its final form a clear, easy-to-follow, and detailed guide for contemplative practice.

# Notes

## Chapter 1: The Instructions for Meditation in Won Buddhism

*Page 3:* [1] *Bhutatathata* is reality as contrasted with unreality or appearance, unchanging or immutable as contrasted with form and phenomena, It is also called self-existent pure Mind, Buddha Nature, *Dharmakaya*, and *Dharma-nature*.

*Page 4:* [2] The Buddha's sitting posture with legs crossed and soles upward, left over right being the attitude for subduing demons, right over left for blessing, the hands being placed one above the other in similar order.

## Chapter 2: The Founding of Won Buddhism and its Historical Backgrounds

*Page 5:* [3] *Tonghak/Donghak*, 'The Eastern Learning' is a religion founded by Choe Je-u in 1860. *Tonghak* venerates *the Lord of Heaven, Haneullim*. Koreans have believed in *Haneullim* from ancient times, thus *Tonghak* could be seen as an authentic Korean religion. accordingly to *Tonghak*, man is not created by a supernatural god but instead is caused by an innate god.

*Page 11:* [4] *Ch'ondogyo*, "Religion of the Heavenly Way," is a twentieth-century Korean religious movement based on Korean folk religion, shamanism, Korean Buddhism, and elements borrowed from Christianity.

## Chapter 3: The Need for Resting in the Elixir Field

*Page 13:* [5] "The elixir field, being the field of the vital force, wards off all diseases. If the mind stops at the elixir field, the vital force and breathing harmonize and thereby cure illness" (*Mohe Zhiguan*, 1911, p.108a).

[6] Korean pronunciation of the Chinese *ch'an-ting*, being the Chinese rendering of the Sanskrit *dhyāna samādhi*. Zen, being *dhyāna* as an element of *samādhi*, covers the whole ground of meditation, concentration, abstraction, reaching the ultimate beyond emotion or thinking. The main characteristic of *sonjong* is serene reflection or clear awareness in the tranquility of no thought.

[7] Meditation practiced with *hwadu*; the same as holding *uidu* (topic of doubt) in meditation.

# Bibliography

Austin, James H. *Zen-Brain reflections*. Cambridge, MA, London, England: The MIT Press, 2006.

Buswell, Robert E., Jr. "Chinul's Systematization of Chinese Meditative Techniques in Korean Son Buddhism," in: *Traditions of Meditation in Chinese Buddhism, Kuroda Institute Studies in East Asian Buddhism 4*, ed. Gregory, P. N. Honolulu, Hawaii: University of Hawaii Press, 1986.

—— "Buddhism in Korea," in: *Buddhism and Asian History*, eds. Kitagawa J.M., and Cummings, M., p.157. Macmillan, 1987.

Chiesa A. Zen meditation: an integration of current evidence. *J. Altern. Complement. Med.* 15(5) (2009): 585-92.

Chih-I, *Stopping and Seeing: A Comprehensive Course in Buddhist Meditation*. Translated by Thomas Cleary. Boston: Shambala Publications, Inc., 1997.

Chon, Pal Khn, trans., *Scriptures of Won-Buddhism (Won pulkyo kyojun)*, Second revised edition. Iri: Won Kwang Publishing Co., 1988.

Chung, Bongkil, *The Scriptures of Won-Buddhism: A Translation of the Wonbulgyo kyojon with Introduction. A Kuroda Institute Book*, Honolulu, Hawaii: University of Hawaii Press, 2003.

—— Scripture of Sot'aesan, Taejonggyong, in: *The Scriptures of Won-Buddhism: A Translation of the Wonbulgyo kyojon with Introduction. A Kuroda Institute Book*, Honolulu, Hawaii: University of Hawaii Press, 2003.

—— *Wonbulgyo kyosa*. Pt. I, chap. 3, sec.1. in: *The Scriptures of Won-Buddhism: A Translation of the Wonbulgyo kyojon with Introduction. A Kuroda Institute Book*, Honolulu, Hawaii: University of Hawaii Press, 2003.

Chwasan, Ven., The Fourth Head Dharma Master of Won Buddhism. 정전 좌선의 방법 해설 *(Chongjon Chawasoneu BangBup Haesul)* [*Commentary on the Method of Sitting Meditation in Chongjon: The Principal Book of Won Buddhism.*] Iksan-si: Won Kwang Publishing Co., 2006.

Cleary, Thomas, trans., "Anthology on the Cultivation of Realization." in: *Taoist Meditation*, 7-80. Boston: Shambala Publications, 2000.

—— "Secret Writings on the Mechanisms of Nature." in: *Taoist Meditation*, 112-116. Boston: Shambala Publications, 2000.

—— "Taiji Alchemy Secrets." in: *Taoist Meditation*, 117-122. Boston: Shambala Publications, 2000.

—— "Treatise on Sitting Forgetting." in: *Taoist Meditation*, 81-105. Boston: Shambala Publications, 2000.

Creswell JD, Myers HF, Cole SW, Irwin MR. "Mindfulness meditation training effects on CD4+ T lymphocytes in HIV-1 infected adults: a small randomized controlled trial." *Brain Behav. Immun.* 23(2) (2009): 184-8.
Dumoulin, Heinrich, *Zen Buddhism: A History. Vol.2, Japan*, Translated by J.W. Heisig and P. Knitter. New York: Macmillan Publishing company, London: Collier Macmillan Publishers, 1990.
Dürckheim, Karlfried Graf, *Hara. The Vital Center of Man*, Translated by Sylvia-Monica von Kospoth. Rochester, Vermont: Inner Traditions, 2004.
Himelstein S. "Meditation Research: The State of the Art in Correctional Settings." *Int. J. Offender Ther. Comp. Criminol.* 55(4) (2011): 646-61.
Maciocia G. *The Foundations of Chinese Medicine. A Comprehensive Text for Acupuncturists and Herbalists.* Second Edition. Elsevier, 2005.
Murphy M. and Donovan S. *The Physical and Physiological Effects of Meditation: A Review of Contemporary Meditation Research with a Comprehensive Bibliography 1931-1996.* Ed. Taylor E., 2nd edition. Inst. of Noetic Sciences, 1997.
Newberg AB, Wintering N, Waldman MR, Amen D, Khalsa DS, Alavi A. "Cerebral blood flow differences between long-term meditators and non-meditators." *Conscious Cogn.* 19(4) (2010): 899-905.
Olivo EL. "Protection throughout the life span: the psychoneuro-immunologic impact of Indo-Tibetan meditative and yogic practices." *Ann. N.Y. Acad. Sci.* 1172 (2009): 163-71.
Park, Kwangsoo, "Sot'aesan's Essays on the Reformation of Korean Buddhism." *Intl. J. of Buddhist Thought and Culture* 3 (2003): 169-94.
Robinet, Isabelle. *Taoist meditation: the Mao-shan tradition of great purity.* Translated by Julian F Pas and Norman J Girardot. Albany, NY: State University of New York Press, 1993.
Rosenzweig S, Greeson JM, Reibel DK, Green JS, Jasser SA, Beasley D. "Mindfulness-based stress reduction for chronic pain conditions: variation in treatment outcomes and role of home meditation practice." *J. Psychosom. Res.* 68(1) (2010): 29-36.
Sotaesan (Park Chung-Bin), *Choson pulgyo hyokshillon (Essays on the Reformation of Korean Buddhism).* Translated by Kwangsoo Park, San Francisco: International Scholars Press, 1997.
Sudsuang R, Chentanez V, Veluvan K. "Effect of Buddhist meditation on serum cortisol and total protein levels, blood pressure, pulse rate, lung volume and reaction time." *Physiol. Behav.* 50(3) (1991): 543-8.
T'ien T'ai, Chih-I. *Mohe Zhiguan* (Ch. 摩訶止観) 8, *Taisho shinshu daizokyo* 46, Tokyo, 1911, p.108a.

Witek-Janusek L, Albuquerque K, Chroniak KR, Chroniak C, Durazo-Arvizu R, Mathews HL. "Effect of mindfulness based stress reduction on immune function, quality of life and coping in women newly diagnosed with early stage breast cancer." *Brain Behav. Immun.* 22(6) (2008): 969-81.

Zeidan F, Johnson SK, Diamond BJ, David Z, Goolkasian P. "Mindfulness meditation improves cognition: evidence of brief mental training." *Conscious Cogn.* 19(2) (2010): 597-605.

# INDEX

*Anthology on the Cultivation of Realization*, 20, 24, 27-9, 31, 39
anxiety, 34
Āryadeva, 8
asymmetry, 34
attention, 4, 16, 21, 26, 31, 34
Austin, J.H., 33, 39
*Avataṃsaka Sūtra*, 8
awareness, 17, 23, 34, 38

Bai Yuzhan, 24
*Benefits of Meditation*, 33
bladder, 25
bliss, 4, 32-33
blood, 4, 13, 25-26, 30, 34-36, 40
bodily pain, 35
breast cancer, 35, 41
breathing, 4, 21-23, 26, 38
Buddha, 5-11, 15, 19, 21, 28-29, 37-38
    Dharma, 5, 6, 10-11
    Nature, 28, 38
    Śākyamuni, 6
    teachings of the, 5-9, 37
Buddhahood, 13
Buddhist, 1-2, 5-12, 14, 18, 20-21, 29, 34-35, 37, 39-40
    meditation, 1, 34-35, 39-40
    offering, 9
    principles, 6
    teaching, 1, 5-6, 12, 21
Buswell, R.E., Jr., 5, 8, 39

calm in wakefulness, 4, 27
calmness, 4, 13-14, 27-29, 34
    of Zen, 13
cancer, 34-35, 41
*Canon*, 2, 12, 29
Cáodòng (Ts'ao-tung) School, 9
*caudate*, 34
*Center for Buddhist Studies at the University of California, Los Angeles (UCLA)*, 5
cerebral blood flow (CBF), 34, 40
Ch'an, 9, 18, 21
*ch'i*, 26
Ch'ondogyo, 11, 15, 38
*Ch'u-tz'u*, 26-27
Chiesa, A., 35, 39
Chih-I (Zhiyi), 12, 15, 39
*chin-chiang*, 27
*Chin-kang ching*, 15
*chin-li*, 27
China, 7-9, 11, 17
Chinan, 10
Chinese medicine, 24-25, 40
Chinul, 9, 39
Chongsan, 5
*Choosing Mindful Actions*, 9
Choson dynasty, 8
Christianity, 5, 15, 38
chronic pain, 34-35, 40
Chung, Bongkil, 2-3, 6, 9-12, 15-16, 26, 33, 39-40
Chwasan, 15-18, 21-23, 28-31, 39
compassion, 34
*Compendium of Buddhism*, 15

# Index

*Compendium of Eastern Learning*, 15
concentration, 4, 10, 13, 20-22, 24, 32, 38
Confucian, 11, 31
Confucianism, 5, 15
*Contemplation into Facts and Principles*, 9
*Contemporary Studies on Meditation*, 33
cortisol, 35, 40
Creswell, J.D., 35, 40
criminal offenders, 34
cross-legged position, 16
*Cultivation of Realization*, 20, 24, 27, 29, 31, 39
*Cultivation of Spirituality*, 9-10
CV6 of the meridian points in acupuncture, 12

*Dan Tian/Tantien/Dandien*, 2
delusive thoughts, 3-4, 20, 22, 27, 29, 31, 39
*Dhammakāya*, 35
*Diamond Sutra*, 6, 15
*divine juice*, 27
Doctrinal School, 8, 10
Dōgen Kigen, 15-16, 32
Donovan S., 36, 40
drowsiness, 4, 22-23, 28
Dumoulin, H., 15-16, 22, 32, 40
Dürckheim, K.G., 18-19, 40
*Dvadasanikāya Śāstra*, 8

*Eight Aspects of the Buddha's Life*, 15
electroencephalography (EEG), 34
*elixir field*, 2, 4, 12-13, 17, 24, 38
emptiness, 12

energy, 2-4, 12-13, 17-18, 21-24, 26, 31
circulation, 23
fiery, 3-4, 13, 21, 24, 26
vital, 12
watery, 3-4, 24, 26
enlightenment, 5-6, 10, 15, 37
*Essentials of Zen*, 15
executive functioning, 34
eyes closed, 4, 22-23

*Filial Piety*, 15
*Fixed-Term and Daily Training*, 11
*Flower Garland Sutra*, 8
*Flowery Lake*, 26-27
*Foundations of Chinese Medicine*, 24, 40
Founder of Won Buddhism, 2, 5
*Four Classics*, 15
*Fukanzazengi*, 32
*fukubu*, 12
*Furnace of Creation*, 24

*Gate of Life*, 25
*Gate of Practice, or Discipline*, 9
*gold liqueur*, 27
*golden beverage*, 27

hand mudra, 17
*hara*, 12, 18-19, 40
Head Dharma Master of Won Buddhism
Founding, 11-12, 23, 37
Fourth, 15-17, 21, 23, 28, 39
Second, 5
health-related quality of life (HRQoL), 35
heart, 19, 24-25, 34

Himelstein, S., 34, 40
HIV-1, 25, 40
*honored middle*, 12
*Hsiao-Ching*, 15
*hsuan-chuan*, 27
*Huang-t'ing Ching*, 26-27
*Huayan (Hua-yen)* school, 8
*hwadu*, 9-10, 13, 38
*Hymns*, 15

illness, 13, 17, 21, 33-34, 38
immune function, 35, 41
incantation, 9-10
India, 7
inner alchemy, 24, 26
*Instructions for Meditation in Won Buddhism*, 1-3, 5, 26, 29, 37
intoning the name of Buddha, 9-10
itching, 30
itchy, 4, 30

*jade*
  *beverage*, 27
  *juice*, 27
  *sap*, 27
  *pond*, 13
*Jade Hinge*, 15
Japanese, 9, 12, 15, 18-19

Kabat-Zinn, J., 34
*kanhwa*, 9
*kanhwa-Son*, 13
karmic retribution, 10
*Kasa*, 15
kidneys, 24-25
*kikai*, 12
*koan*, 5, 9-10
Koguryŏ, 8
*kongan*, 10
Korea, 5-8, 21, 39

Korean Buddhism, 6-8, 17, 38, 40
*kungan*, 9

*li-ch'uan*, 27
life span, 36, 40
*ling-i*, 27
*Línjì (Lin-chi)* School, 8
*Lotus Sutra*, 8
*lower burner*, 25

Maciocia, G., 24-25, 40
*Mādhyamika Śāstra*, 8
magnetic resonance imaging (MRI), 34
*Mahāvaipulya Buddhāvataṃsaka Sūtra*, 8
Mandok Mountain, 10
*Meditation-Only* School, 7-8
mental decoction, 13
midbrain, 34
mind, 1, 3-4, 10, 13, 17-31, 34, 38
mind-body interactions, 34
*Mindful Choice in Action*, 10
Mindfulness, 1, 28-29, 34-35, 40-41
  meditation, 34-35, 40-41
  practice, 34
*Mindfulness-Based Stress Reduction (MBSR) Program*, 34-35, 40
*ming men*, 25
*Mo-ho chih-kuan (Mohe Zhiguan)*, 12, 15, 38, 40
mouth, 3-4, 23-24, 26
Murphy, M., 36, 40
*Mutual Support of Fire and Water*, 25
*Heart and Kidneys*, 25

mysterious
    manifestations, 31
    phenomena, 31
*mysterious source*, 27

Nāgārjuna, 8
Neurochemistry, 34
Newberg, A.B., 34, 40
North Cholla Province, 10
*nourishment of immortality*, 26

*o-naka*, 12
oedema, 18, 25
Olivo, E.L., 36, 40
*One Hundred Verses Treatise*, 8
*original nature*, 3-4, 27-29, 31-33
Orthodox School, 8

*P'alsangjon*, 15
Paekche, 8
pain, 4, 16-18, 29-30, 34-35, 40
    in the legs, 4, 29
Pak Chung-Bin, 2
Pal Khn Chon, 16, 39
parietal cortex, 34
path of inner refinement, 24
pelvis, 17
posture, 4, 15-18, 29, 38
*Power of Inquiry into Facts and Principles*, 10
    *Meditation*, 10
    *Mindful Choice*, 10
practices of Inquiry, Cultivation, and Mindful Choice, 10
*prajñā*, 10
prefrontal cortex, 34

pressure, 35, 40
    diastolic, 35
    systolic, 35
psychic powers, 31
*Pulbop yon'guhoe*, 6
*Pulgyo Taejon*, 15
pulse rate, 35, 40
*pure water of the jade lake*, 27
*Purport*, 2-3
putamen, 34

*Qi*, 25
quality of life (QOL), 35

recidivism, 34
reformed Buddhist movement, 5
rehabilitation, 35
*Research Society of Buddha Dharma*, 6
right thought, 4, 27
*Rinzai*, 9
Robinet, I., 26, 40
Rosenzweig, S., 33, 40

saliva, 4, 13, 24, 26-27
salivary
    duct, 13
    gland, 4, 24
*samādhi*, 10, 28, 38
*Saṃgha*, 10
*Śata Śāstra*, 7
Schools of Korean Buddhism, 8
*Scripture of Sot'aesan*, 6, 9-11, 15, 26, 39
*Scripture on the Nourishment of the Vital Principle and the Prolongation of Life*, 27
*Scriptures of Won-Buddhism*, 1-3, 12, 39

*Secret Planning*, 15
*Secret Writings on the
   Mechanisms of Nature*, 22,
   24, 39
*sedate belly*, 19
shamanic, 11
shamanism, 11
*shen*, 24
*Śīla*, 10
*simmdan*, 13
*Sitting in Meditation*, 2-4, 10,
   12-13, 19, 29, 31-33
*Six Articles to Heed
   in Daily Applications*, 11
   *while Attending the Temple
   throughout the Daily
   Training*, 11
six sense organs, 3, 33
*skillful-means*, 7
sleepiness, 22-23, 28
small intestine, 24-25
Song Kyu, 5
*sonjong*, 13, 38
*Sonyo*, 15
Sot'aesan, 2, 5-13, 15, 17,
   23, 26-28, 30-31, 33, 37,
   39-40
*Sōtō*, 9
*source of jade*, 27
SPECT imaging, 34
*Spirit produces energy and energy
   produces spirit*, 24
spleen, 24-25
stress, 34-36, 40-41
*Stress Reduction Clinic*, 34
substance use, 34
Sudsuang, R., 35, 40
Suei Dynasty, 8
supernatural occurrences,
   31
*sweet source*, 27

T'ao Hung-ching, 27
T'ien T'ai, Chih-I, 12, 40
*T'ien-T'ai (Tiantai)* School,
   12
*Ta-tung chen-Ching*, 26
*Taejonggyong*, 6, 9-11, 15, 26,
   39
*Taiji Alchemy Secrets*, 23-24,
   39
*tanden*, 12
Tang Dynasty, 9
*Tanjon/Danjeon*, 2, 4, 12-13,
   17-18, 21-22, 24
Taoism, 5, 11-12, 15, 18, 20-
   21, 24, 26, 37
Taoist, 11-13, 17, 20-27, 29,
   31, 39-40
Testaments, Old and New,
   11, 15
thalamus, 34
*Three Great Practices*, 10
Three Kingdoms, 8
three major attributes of
   Buddhist practice, 9
*Three Treatises*, 8
Threefold Training of
   Buddhism, 9
*Tonggyong Taejon*, 15
*Tonghak*, 5, 38
torpor, 28
*Treatise of Treatises*, 7
*Treatise on Sitting Forgetting*,
   17, 20, 39
*True Thusness*, 3-4, 14, 27-28,
   32
true void, 29
*Twelve Gates Treatise*, 8

*uidu*, 10, 38
*upaya*, 7
uterus, 25

visualization, 36
visuo-spatial processing, 34
vital
    energy, 12
    force, 3, 13, 26, 38

*Wai-Ching*, 26
*wakeful in calmness*, 4, 27
wandering thoughts, 20, 28
Wang Chongyang, 24
*water arising and fire descending*, 13
*water-of-life*, 26
*Way of Perfect Truthfulness*, 31
*Way of the Fourfold Beneficence*, 10
wholehearted sitting, 9
Witek-Janusek, L., 35, 41
*Won* Buddhism, 1-3, 5-6, 9, 11-12, 15-17, 21-23, 26, 28-29, 31, 33, 37-39
*Wonbulgyo*, 3, 5, 39
working memory, 34

*yang*, 24-25
Yao, 27
Yi, Kwang Jung, 15
*yin*, 24-25
*Yin-fu Ching*, 15
Yoga, 15, 34
*yu-ch'uan*, 27
*yu-chiang*, 27
*yu-chin*, 27
*yu-i*, 27
*Yu-shu Ching*, 15
*yu-tz'u ch'ing-shui*, 27
*Yuan-Ch'i*, 27

*Zazen*, 15, 22, 32
Zeidan, F., 34, 41
Zen, 1, 10, 13, 15-18, 21-23, 33-35, 38-40
    illness, 21
    practice, 34
    timeless, 1
*Zen-Brain Reflections*, 33, 39
Zhiyi, 12

# About the Author

Dr. Serge V. Yarovoi is a scientist, poet, translator, and meditation teacher. He holds an MS degree in biochemistry, a PhD in chemistry, and a master's degree in applied meditation studies. He works at the Perelman School of Medicine at the University of Pennsylvania in Philadelphia, Pennsylvania. He has authored multiple publications in the biomedical sciences and is also known for his poetry publications in a variety of internationally renowned journals and periodicals.